THE SCHEMES OF SATAN

THE ENEMY OF MAN

WORK TO DEFEAT

THE G-D CONSCIOUS

بسم الله الرحمن الرحيم

BOOKLET

ISBN 9781097214853

بسم الله الرحمن الرحيم

CONTENTS

بسم الله الرحمن الرحيم

In a 3-year period **Imam W. Deen Mohammed** led and oversaw the largest mass conversion to Islam in the history of the United States of America. He forged close ties with Muslim communities worldwide and established strong relationships with many of the world's faiths and their prominent leadership.

Imam W. Deen Mohammed, leader of the largest community of Muslims in the United States of America passed on September 9, 2008. We pray that his work continues to grow and serve humanity as he would have desired it to, through all of us who have benefited so greatly from his teachings. Ameen

Structure, Guard and Publish the Knowledge

"We need knowledge, then we need protection for it. How do you protect knowledge? Some people say, "You protect knowledge by not letting anybody interfere with it. Don't let anybody change it. Publish it! When you publish it, people know it. That's its protection." Yes! If you want to protect your knowledge, publish it! When you publish it, it is protected and the people know it. But if you keep it locked up to yourself, you will die, and your knowledge will die with you. Or your enemy will get a hold to it and he will publish it after you in a corrupt form.

Thus, Allah swt says. "And We have revealed it for the express purpose that it should be propagated." Yes! That is its guarantee that it will be protected. When it's propagated in its right form, then the people will inherit it directly. They don't have to listen to what you have to say. You won't have to tell them what Prophet Muhammad (pbuh) said, they got it directly. It was published by him in his lifetime.

If we want to guard the knowledge that we have, we must publish it. The more people know about it, the more it is guaranteed that it will live, and it won't be changed. The less people know about it, the better the chance that it will die with us or be changed. Yes! We structure the knowledge and we propagate the knowledge."
Imam W. Deen Mohammed

بسم الله الرحمن الرحيم

Abbreviations Clarified

G-d for God
In this book the word God is written as G-d for the respect of the word "god" because some people mirror to disrespect it with the word "dog."

swt for Subhana Wa Tallah
The abbreviation after Allah swt means "Subhana Wa Tallah" in Arabic which means "The Sacred and The Mighty" in English.

(PBUH) for Peace Be Upon Him
The abbreviation after Prophet Muhammad (pbuh) means "May the Peace and Blessings of Allah G-d be upon him" in English and "Sal Allahu Allahi Wa Salaam" in Arabic.

AS for Alayhi Salam
The abbreviation AS means "Alayhi Salaam" in Arabic, which means "May Allah G-d bless him" in English.

Imam W Deen Mohammed
Salatul Jumuah Khutbah
Chicago, IL
January 3, 2003

Imam W. Deen Mohammed

Dear Believers, Muslims, As-Salaam-Alaikum.
With Allah's Name, The Gracious, The
Compassionate, Beneficent Benefactor, The
Merciful Benefactor and The Merciful Redeemer,
we witness that He is One, The Creator of the
Heavens and the Earth. That there is no partner
with Him in the rule of the Heavens and the
Earth; He is G-d Alone.

And we witness that Muhammed is His Servant
and His Messenger, Prayers and Peace be upon
him and what follows of that traditional salutation
to the Last Prophet, The Seal of the Prophets,
mentioned in the Qur'an as being the liberator
coming to purify the people and to bring them out
of darkness of ignorance, corruption and slavery
into the Light of G-d's Truth.

In the Qur'an, Allah says that he, Prophet
Muhammed (PBUH), is the one mentioned in

The Torah, the Old Books of the Bible, as the one coming to purify you and take off your back the heavy yoke that weighed you down and to break every bond of slavery.

We think of slavery in the physical sense readily, but the worst form of slavery is not the slavery of the physical body. The worst form of enslavement is the enslavement of your soul, when you don't have your soul free for yourself.

Your mind and your heart can all be enslaved by the Satan, Shaitan, the enemy of all human beings. He is the enemy of the human family. Allah says of him, "Fight the schemes of Satan." His plots, deceitful tricks plan to defeat you in your purposes, in your best life and in your best hopes for life.

Satan is out to defeat you right there, so you will be seen as ridiculous. He loves to make human

beings ridiculous. And the ones whom he wants most to bring down and make ridiculous are those who support the Scriptures of G-d, the religious people. He wants to make them look ridiculous.

If we understand the Scriptures, the Qur'an and the Bible which was before the Qur'an was revealed, about Satan's hopes and aspirations, we have to understand that according to these Holy Books and Sacred Scriptures, Satan's hope was to finally deceive people in the best places of their religious world the holy sanctuaries, in the most sacred places.

Satan had a plan to defeat the Christians in their most sacred beliefs and in their most sacred places. And Satan has a plan to defeat the Muslims in our most sacred places. And Satan has been successful; he has discredited religion and brought religion to be a ridiculous thing in the minds of many decent and intelligent people. They will tolerate religion and won't speak out against it, unless it is with friends like themselves. Then some, like during the spread of Communist ideas in America, openly attacked religion and said, "religion is the opium of the masses of the people." The masses mean the common people. Opium is a drug, and they meant that religion is nothing but something to drug you.

They denied G-d in their ideas and in their planning of their life on this earth. The Communist people did that. They had no place for G-d in their planning. And if you belonged to the Communist order in a Communist society under Communist authority, you could not practice your religion. For 70 plus years, Muslims were not allowed to identify themselves publicly under the Communist Party of Russia.

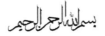

It was only when their power broke and they had to change their ideas, that the Muslims could come out openly and begin to identify as Muslims again and to go to the mosques and pray again. Seventy some years is a long time to be locked away from your religion, kept from practicing your religion where others would witness it.

The Muslim's story is that they would be watched at night. Homes would be looked into, to see if they could catch someone practicing his religion. Muslims would have to stand watch while they prayed at night. They continued to practice their religion secretly, and that is wonderful. Someone would have to watch while the family would be having Islamic study lessons.

I'm sure they had to do it very quietly, sometimes whispering, unable to speak aloud, fearing that some device would pick up their activities. Satan inspired the Communist idea.

Some things close to us that are very detrimental and destructive in our lives, we forget that they are from Satan, that they are the schemes and plans of Satan against the life of the human being. Allah says, "Surely, the intoxicants and gambling and games of superstitions are corruptions, of the works of Satan, therefore stay away from such."

As Muslims we cannot drink or take intoxicants. The Arabic word does not say liquid and does not say solid, it only says intoxication, whatever will intoxicate your mind. When the believers were invited to Islam, they were not told immediately to stop drinking. It was the custom of the people to drink.

So look how wonderful Allah is in correcting man in his ways. He is not like us. Right away, we want to tell people what the law is, and we haven't even educated them yet. You haven't even made them aware of the trouble that made necessary the law.

Allah, The Merciful G-d Who loves His human creation, the human beings that He created, first wants to condition you to understand the problem. Then once you understand the problem, He brings to you the prohibition, the law.

Muslims were coming to prayer, can you believe it, intoxicated, under the influence of alcohol or some drugs. You may think that reefers are new, but people have been smoking reefer for longer than the Indians have been having powwows. They called it hashish in Arabic or grass.

It was finally after Muhammed the Prophet (PBUH) had taught them and educated them and got them into another mind, that G-d revealed and told them that intoxicants are of the works of the devil and to stay away from them. It did not come all at once. The first order said, "Do not come to prayer intoxicated." Finally, it came and abolished it all together, saying, "It is the works of Satan and stay away from them." Then it was prohibited.

It was also the same for gambling. And look at how the world gambles now today; it is so popular. In Christianity and in the Bible, the person who gambles is described as a bad person or a weak person. The person who drinks, in the Bible, is described as a weak person and as trouble for the society.

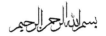

Imam W. Deen Mohammed

Where the Bible doesn't condemn it outright,
clearly like the Qur'an, it does condemn it, if you
study the whole Bible. You will see that drunks
are among the sinners and among the people who
have fallen from the way. We know the Bible
says, "take a little bit for your stomach's sake,"
but that is speaking to the practice of the people
back in those days who used liquors for certain
cures.

Today, you will have certain prescriptions or
remedies prescribed that will have an alcohol
content in them. Also they apply it for cleaning.
There were hygiene and medical purposes for
alcohol, but that did not mean for you to take it.

The eating of swine or pork meat is strictly
forbidden in the Qur'an, but it is also forbidden in
the Bible. And there are many Christians who are

not following the wide-open way of those who walk the wide-open path.

They follow those who are in the narrow arid straight path, and they don't even eat pork. There are Seventh Day Adventists and other Christians who don't eat pork. So don't be deceived by the looks of this world. The looks of this world is what Satan wants you to see. And he wants you to think that all people are like that picture you are looking at, but no.

There are Christians, Jews, Muslims and other people, too, who stay away from those things that corrupt and bring down the society, the people. Look at what the Communist had to do. They condemned religion as the opium of the masses, as drugs for the common people. But as soon as they got into power, they had to stop crime. They stopped the people from drinking as freely as they did before.

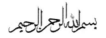

The Communists had to do this. Any people who want to control their public to achieve important things or important objectives or ends, they have to protect the people from the life that corrupts them and brings them down and makes trouble for their families and for the society.

We live in America, and it is not a country that imposes laws upon your private life, but it does impose laws upon your public life. You can drink. But if you drink and drive, you are in trouble with the law if they catch you. You can gamble. But if you gamble without a permit and you are caught, you are in trouble with the law.

There are controls. It is not Islamic, but their society still is telling us that these things are harmful, and if not controlled, the whole country or whole people can be brought down by these things.

Look how cigarettes have troubled the society. They have discovered that they are cancer causing. But not only cigarettes, liquors also can cause cancer and destruction of your organs. But no one is trying to control liquor like they are trying to control cigarettes.

If you look at the world, don't just see these things, study these things, and you will see the schemes of Satan are alcoholism in the society, the sale of drugs. All of these have to be identified as the schemes of Satan, because G-d says, "these are the works of Shaitan," the intoxicants.

Also the promotion of free sex is the scheme of Satan. They would have you to believe that what

you do with your body is your business and you have no one to answer to.

They don't say what you do with your body is your business, except whereas religion is concerned or what G-d says. No, they don't leave any chance for you to think of an Authority to govern your life, but yourself. They make you think you are free, and nothing should govern what you do with your own personal life. That this is your business.

They are saying, if you want to kill yourself, then kill yourself. If you want to corrupt your life, then corrupt your life. If you want to abort your baby, sister, woman or girl, abort your baby; that is your business, that's your body.

Why do I identify this as the schemes of Satan? G-d wants to bring together those things that should be together. G-d created those things that belong together, to be together and to be brought together, if they are not together, and to stay together like husband, wife, family. G-d created family to be together and to stay together. Satan wants to break families up.

This scheme of Satan, perhaps, is the scheme that all the other schemes can be seen under or this one scheme can reveal all of the other schemes. What I am talking about is his scheme to break up that which should be together, to divide that which should be united, to separate that which should be together.

To break up families is one of the objects of the Satan. That is what he has to do, because if he doesn't break up families, then there is an authority in the life of the people. Family is an organization. Family is an institution. The whole

Imam W. Deen Mohammed

---

society has been built upon the institutions we call family.

The family is the mother of all other units of society. Family mothered all other units of society. It is deserving of a discussion in detail. When he divides the family, the father has no authority, no voice in the house. The mother has no authority or no voice in the house. The children in the family are all separated, and the family is disunited.

Then when Satan makes his appeal, who do the children turn to, to see if he should be obeyed or not? Nobody turns to anybody in the house to see if they should obey the invitation of Satan, when that family is disunited and the members have no respect for the parents, for the father, for the mother, then the voice of Satan can come in easily.

They talk about how great the society is and how wonderful this democracy is. But if you look at the opportunity given to Satan in this democracy, you will see that this democracy is beautiful on the one hand and very ugly on the other. To tell people love your family, is one voice in the society. It says care about your children; did you hug your child today? All of that is beautiful.

But while I am at work, the TV is on, and you are selling my children things that I don't approve of, without my permission. To me, that is total disrespect for family life, for the parent, for the husband, for the wife, for family life.

It is a total disrespect that you will come and appeal to my children before me and in my absence to get them to buy something, whether it is a hamburger or a soda pop or a toy or an item of clothing. I don't care what it is. No appeal

should be made to minors. It should only be made to adults.

When they open up with their commercials, the first thing they should say is "Daddy, may I have your attention?" or "Daddy and momma, may I have your attention?" Then give the commercial. That protects the family. That tells the child that he or she is not to buy this thing or accept this, unless my momma and daddy say OK.

But no, they go directly to every individual in the household, in the family, to sell things as though no one in the household is a minor, as if everyone is a grown up or an adult and can do things independently, can make independent decisions. This is terrible, and this is why we have the society we have right now. Allah wants us to fight the schemes of Satan.

G-d doesn't tell us to go after Satan. That is not the way to find Satan. Satan doesn't have a sharp nose, white skin, blue eyes and yellow hair. Satan is not red skinned with horns sticking out of his head. A picture won't take you to Satan, unless it is a picture of his schemes.

We don't care who started the fire, just let us put it out. Maybe we will catch the one who started it later. That is the way you catch Satan; you put out his fires. That is what Allah wants us to do. If we put out his fires, we put him out of business. That is what Allah wants us to do to put Satan out of business.

Put out Satan's fires of drugs, alcoholism, sex abuse, etc. all these crimes and all this corruption in our lives. Let us fight corruption and evil. Let us fight cruelty. Let us fight lies and falsehoods. Allah has told us in the Qur'an that this is the way He wants us to defeat Satan.

I want you to look at our own people and see how we are helping the devil. Allah says the spendthrifts are the brothers of the devil. Are you in the habit of just spending money and not taking care of your most important needs to see that your phone bill is paid, to see that your lights are kept on, that the heat is on or in the summer, the air conditioner is running, the rent is paid or mortgage note is paid, all of those important things that represent your security for your comfort?

See that they are being paid. Then if you have extra money to spend, don't forget the future. For Allah tells us to be orientated future wise, not just for the present. Muhammed the Prophet told us to take care of how we live today, so that we don't have trouble tomorrow, the prayers and the peace be upon the Prophet.

I know you love Allah, you love this religion. You love G-d's model human person for us, prayers and peace be on him. So if you love those things, how can you stand to behave and live as a brother of the devil and not be bothered by that? You should be bothered by that.

You and your family will sit to the table and eat, and the whole meal that you served, the food that you ate, weighed 10 pounds and five pounds of it went into the garbage. Then you are working with the devil. You have no room in your closet for clothes. You go downstairs in the basement and you are stumbling over clothes. There are clothes everywhere, because you have a buying habit, you just have to buy things.

Spendthrifts are the brothers of the devil. Those who spend without a conscious, who spend without control over their spending, are brothers

of the devil. How are you helping the devil, when you spend that way? The devil wants to take all of your energies in your life away from G-d.

If the devil can keep you under debt and keep you struggling to pay for things, he has tied up your life. He has taken your time from G-d. Look how we have to have two and three in a household working, or more. Some will have two and three part time jobs to make up for one full time job and a half. Some will have two full time jobs. So when they see each other, they are in a hurry, one is rushing to bed and the other rushing to work. They pass each other brushing their teeth.

You don't have time to read the Qur'an enough. You don't have time to reflect enough. To reflect, is what keeps people alive. What is reflecting? It is thinking on the beauty and greatness of G-d, how He made the world so wonderful in its beauty and its goodness. It is how He made animals and plants so wonderful to think on. That gives life to your soul. That gives life to your insides and makes your good insides come alive.

The devil does not want you fed by this healthy food that Allah has created. He wants to keep you so busy, that you don't have time for it. So if you want to get more time, brothers and sisters, stop spending on things that you don't have to have. Stop eating on more than you can consume. Know that it is a sin to bite off a piece of chicken and then throw it in the garbage, that is a sin.

I know some brothers and sisters will eat with their family in a restaurant and know that they can't control the situation, because Satan's influences are too powerful, his schemes are too powerful. So the brother will order very little from the menu, probably toast and a cup of coffee. Then when the rest of them finish, he'll

ask, "Are you finished?" Then he goes and eats chicken and half a cheeseburger and will be full, because what they left is more than enough to fill him up.

I'd rather see a brother do that, than for a family to waste their hard-earned money. If a hamburger costs $1 and you throw half of it in the garbage, then you threw 50 cents into the garbage. If the drink costs 60 cents and you throw half of it in the garbage.... and some will throw all of it in the garbage, just like they are not poor.

You should go to the homes of the rich and see how they eat. I would say sit in their neighborhoods quietly, but you may get arrested.... and on garbage pickup day, see how much garbage is picked up in their neighborhoods. Then come back to our neighborhoods and see how much garbage is collected, it is horrible.

The garbage truck is taking your money away. You are hiring more and more garbage scavengers than anyone else. The city has to hire more garbage pickup men for you, so your sewage bill for the city is higher than the rich person's bill. Does that make sense?

The devil, the Satan, also inspired slavery, to give their souls and their bodies to a man who can buy them, who can pay for their soul. Satan says, "Now we can't do this ugly thing anymore and make people, who have not done a crime work for nothing anymore." They call them slaves, so we have to let their bodies free. Then he devises something else for you.

You are not slaves on a plantation with your movements restricted, but he has done something

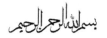

that created the same results or effect. What he wanted was the total control of your life, and that is what he has gotten by hooking you with commercialism, by hooking you with consumer spending and hooking you with his devices of intoxicants and sexual corruption. He doesn't have to worry about the masses of people, for he has enslaved them all.

I return to what I have said in the beginning. There are many forms to slavery, and sometimes the worst form of slavery is not the enslavement of your physical body but the enslavement of your soul. G-d says: "Oh you who believe, save your own souls and your families from the fire."

We ask Allah to forgive us our sins and our weaknesses. Oh Allah, save us from our own weaknesses and purify us and do not let our hearts go back to corruption, after You have guided us aright, Ameen.

Let us remember the requirements for Muslim life and the proof for Muslim life. The requirement for Muslim life is that we obey G-d's instructions. That we violate none of His commands. Whatever He orders, we obey.

If we should fall and become weak or forget and Satan slips something in on us, the moment that we recognize that we are out of the form that Allah wants us in, we ask forgiveness, so that we can get back in the form Allah created us for, the form of a Muslim believing in G-d. Remember also that faith is the first life. Knowledge gives structure, design and much growth to the life. But the life is faith. Faith is the first life and it is *the life*. If you take faith out of it, it dies. The whole life dies.

No matter how great the knowledge is to structure the life and to advance the life and increase the life in so many wonderful things, if you take faith out, it is like taking water out of the beautiful garden. Then all of the beautiful life will soon die, and it will be gone.

Hold on to your faith and ask Allah to increase you in faith. And we also want Allah to increase us in knowledge. But remember what makes your faith strong. It is remembering Allah, when you are facing trouble. It is remembering Allah when you are enjoying and experiencing great joy in your life. In the two extremes of joy and sorrow, remember Allah.

When there is an occasion for sorrow and an occasion for joy, remember Allah. And your faith will increase, because Allah is going to make His Presence in your life stronger and plainer for you.

If you remember Him, the more you see Him plainly working in your life with you, the more your faith will increase.

Your faith will increase to a point where you will not always want to say you believe, you will say, "Oh, I know that. I know Allah will do that for me. I know my G-d." That is a person who has stayed close to their G-d in faith, for such a long period of time.

They have no more questions about it, they know their G-d and know what their G-d can do. *The people have heard a caller in the land calling to faith, and we have responded saying, we believe, so write us down with the righteous.* Isn't that wonderful? Muhammed the Prophet (PBUH) said, "You will never enter the Garden of Paradise until you have faith, and you will not have faith until you practice love.

We've been told that those not in the flames, will go over it, and see the flames and those mourning, groaning and crying and their pain, because the fire is on them; but they will be passing over safely into the Garden of Paradise, praise be to Allah.

"You will never enter the Garden of Paradise, until you believe." Faith is first. Then he says there is a condition for even having faith. Why do I have faith in my momma? It is because my momma took care of me and protected me and gave me food and came to my rescue. That is why I have faith in my momma. If she had not done those things, I would not have had faith in her.

So what will strengthen or be the condition to cause us to have faith? It is the proof that we love one another. It also said, "You will not have faith, until you practice loving one another." When you practice loving one another, you strengthen the bonds between you and your brother. And because the brother knows that you love him, he believes in you and he trusts you.

Faith is not just a belief; faith also is a trust. *You will not enter the Garden of Paradise, until you have faith, and you will not have faith, until you practice love.* So we thank Allah for His Mercy, the Mercy of the good Muslim life, the natural life that He created for us.

We thank Him for His Mercy of Revelation, the Qur'an, that is Guidance for us to take care of all of our needs in this life for as long as we exist on this planet earth. And we thank Him for His model human being, the one He created for each and every one of us to be in model of Muhammed the Prophet, the prayers and the peace be upon him.

We thank Him for His Word, the Qur'an. These sources are really the sources that make our life and keep our life. Don't ever let anybody take those away from you. And the Satan will want to rob you of everything, so that he will be the only one for you to turn to.

You won't turn to Satan as a person, you will turn to him as a supporter of your way of life. You will turn to his intoxicants, his drugs, his corruption, his division of the family and destruction of the family life. Strengthen yourselves. All the great communities of faith now are stressing the importance of family life and how we have to strengthen our families. This is a battle in these last times to save ourselves and our own lives from Satan.

So let us be with Christians and Jews and Buddhists and Hindus and all good people who are fighting Satan's schemes. They are fighting to keep family life strong and to keep faith in the soul and to keep righteous the life.

We ask Allah to protect for us the Blessings that He has given us, for if He does not protect them, we will certainly lose them. Oh Allah, protect for us the gifts You have given to us, including our good wives and our good husbands and our good children. Let us remember the requirements for Muslim life and the proof for Muslim life. The requirement for Muslim life is that we obey G-d's Instructions. That we violate none of His Commands. Whatever He orders, we obey.

ABOUT IMAM W DEEN MOHAMMED

Imam W. Deen Mohammed was unanimously elected as leader of his community after the passing of his father in 1975; the Honorable Elijah Muhammad, founder, leader, and builder of the Nation of Islam.

At a very early age, Imam Mohammed developed a keen scholastic interest in science, psychology and religion. He began his education, from elementary through secondary school, at the University of Islam in Chicago. Further educational pursuits took him to Wilson Junior College, where he concentrated on microbiology and to the Loop Junior College where he studied English, history, and the social sciences. However, his primary education has come from self-study and through his continued pursuit of religion and social truths.

Imam Mohammed's astute leadership, profound social commentary on major issues, piercing scriptural insight into the Torah, Bible and Quran, and his unique ability to apply scriptural interpretation to social issues have brought him numerous awards and high honors. He is a man of vision who has performed many historical firsts.

In 1992, he delivered the first invocation in the U.S. senate to be given by a Muslim. In 1993 he gave an Islamic prayer at President William Jefferson Clinton's first inaugural interfaith prayer service, and again in 1997 at President Clinton's second inaugural interfaith prayer service. His strong interest in interfaith dialogue led him to address the Muslim-Jewish

conference on March 6, 1995, with leaders of Islam and Reform Judaism in Glencoe, IL. In October of 1996, Imam Mohammed met Pope John Paul, II, at the Vatican, at the invitation of Archbishop William Cardinal Keeler and the Focolare Movement. He met with the Pope again, on October 28, 1999, on the "Eve of the New Millennium" in St. Peter's basilica with many other world religious leaders.

In 1997, the Focolare Movement presented him with the "Luminosa Award," for promoting interfaith dialogue, peace, and understanding in the U.S. In 1999, Imam Mohammed served on the advisory panel for Religious Freedom Abroad, formed by Secretary of State Madeline Albright. He assisted in promoting religious freedom in the United States and abroad. In April, 2005, Imam Mohammed participated in a program that featured, "a conversation with

Imam W. Deen Mohammed and Cardinal George of the Catholic Archdiocese."

There are many more accolades, achievements and accomplishments made by Imam W. Deen Mohammed. His honorary Doctorates, Mayoral, and Gubernatorial Proclamations give testament to his recognized voice, and the benefit of his leadership to Muslims and non-Muslims alike. He was appointed to the World Supreme Council of Mosques because of the value of his work and leadership in America.

Today, the dignity and world recognition Imam Mohammed has generated is seen all across the world.

OTHER TITLES BY
IMAM W. DEEN MOHAMMED
Contact WDM Publications for availability

- Noah's Flood Lecture Series
- Ramadan: Meaning, Blessings, Celebration
- Muslim Unity
- Healthy Consciousness in Society
- Diversity in Al Islam
- Mohammed The Prophet ﷺ | The Perfect Man - The Complete Man
- The Story of Joseph
- And Follow the Best Thereof
- It's Time We Sing A New Song [75 Select Poems]
- Wake Up to Human Life
- Islam The Religion of Peace
- As the Light Shineth From the East
- Life the Final Battlefield
- Message of Concern [Removal of All Images That Attempt to Portray Divine]
- The Teachings of W. D. Muhammad 1975

- The Lectures of Imam W. D. Muhammad 1976
- Book of Muslim Names
- The Man and the Woman in Islam
- Prayer and Al-Islam
- Religion on the Line
- Imam W. Deen Muhammad Speaks from Harlem, N.Y. Book 1
- Imam W. Deen Muhammad speaks from Harlem, N.Y.: Challenges That Face Man Today Book 2
- Meeting the Challenge: Halal Foods for Our Everyday Needs
- An African American Genesis
- Focus on Al-Islam: Interviews with Imam W. Deen Mohammed
- Al-Islam: Unity, and Leadership
- Worst Oppression Is False Worship "The Key Is Tautened-Oneness of Allah
- Growth for a Model Community in America
- Islam's Climate for Business Success
- Mohammed Speaks

- Blessed Ramadan - The Fast of Ramadan
- Plans for a Better Future: Peace, Inclusion and International Brotherhood
- The Schemes of Satan the Enemy of Man
- The Champion We Have in Common: The Dynamic African American Soul
- A Time for Greater Communities Vol. 1-4
- Securing our Share of Freedom
- Return to Innocence: Transitioning of the Nation of Islam

Purchase Copies of This Publication:

WDM Publications
PO Box 1944, Calumet City, IL 60409

Phone: 708-862-7733
Email: wdmpublications@sbcglobal.net

www.WDMPublications.com

For More on Imam W. Deen Mohammed

Ministry of Imam W. Deen Mohammed
PO Box 1061, Calumet City, IL 60409

Phone: 708-679-1587
Email: wdmministry@sbcglobal.net

www.TheMosqueCares.com

Made in the USA
Middletown, DE
13 April 2021